PRESENTS:

DELIVER ME FROM ME

BY: LATOYA EARLY

ACKNOWLEDGEMENTS

This has been an amazing journey writing this book. God has certainly revealed many revelations to me in the mist of developing this project. I'd like to altruistically thank my husband, Demetrious Early. He has allowed me to pursue my dreams as a writer, by encouraging me, motivating me, and loving me. God couldn't have blessed me better. Without his patience and understanding I would not have had the honor to bless my new readers with this Word from God.

Thank you to my Righteous G.I.R.L.'s of The Fountain of Truth, Righteous Youth Church of Detroit, MI, for inspiring me to reach beyond our ministry and strive for greater.

Thank you to my parents, sisters, friends, editors, teachers and my critical reviewers, I love and appreciate you.

A special thank you to those who contributed to my vision,

Bishop Michael Jones Sr. Pastor,
Fountain of Truth Church, Detroit, MI
NG Designs and Prints
MYAN Business Consulting
Doris of C.I.H.I.

DEDICATION

This book is dedicated to young women across the nation. You struggle everyday against the pain of your past and I truly pray you find salvation, deliverance and peace in this reading. Always know, God created you on purpose and there's nothing you can do about it!

CONTENTS

From the Author,

I pray this reading encourages you to be a better you. Lessons of our past can truly hinder our future, if we allow them to cause us to stop believing. I pray that you are able to relate your personal experiences to the monologues in this reading, providing you with a new understanding of how to defeat your past. I pray deliverance takes place during the reading of the passages; deliverance starts first in the heart of the conflicted. I pray that reading this book will ignite your desire to make a life changing decision and causes you to begin to conquer the challenge of living a righteous lifestyle. These things I ask, in Jesus Name, Amen

♥ *Be Blessed xoxo*

Mrs. La'Toya Early,
"A Righteous G.I.R.L."

INTRODUCTION

Being a Christian woman can be a difficult challenge God requires us to conquer. It takes discipline, prayer and motivation to obtain the blessings and peaceful living God has for each and every one of us. "Deliver Me from Me", was written to encourage and inspire young women of all ages, who have experienced challenging situations in their lives. Each section provides a monologue, poetry, prayer and supporting scripture that will encourage each reader to over-come the struggles of their life lessons. We ask God to forgive us for our sins, or wrong doings, but do we honestly forgive ourselves? Are you harboring bad decisions or guilt, which inadvertently could be causing you to miss God's blessings for you? I want to encourage every girl that regardless of your circumstance the God we serve will never leave you nor forsake you as long as you believe that His word will manifest in your life according to your effort.

It has been my heart's desire for several years to provide words of wisdom to girls across the world. I want every girl to know that the enemy tempts every woman to go against the Will of God, *1 Corinthians 10:13 reads; the temptations in your life are no different from what others experience. And God is faithful. He will not allow temptation to be more than you can stand. When you are tempted, He will show you a way out so that you can endure (1 Corinthians 10:13, NLT),* but together we can fight the attacks of the enemy and stand firm in His Word together. The bible teaches us that the power of prayer strengthens in numbers, so the more G.I.R.L.s we have praying in agreement the better our results from God. We must all pray daily for the girl that may be experiencing one of the situations in the reading. We all have experienced some type of challenge in our life, now imagine how much easier it could have been if you were praying for your situation and had other believers praying with you. God has assigned me to minister to young women across the nation by providing examples of how to whole-heartedly apply His principles to your lives and declare the lifestyle of "A Righteous G.I.R.L.".

A Righteous G.I.R.L. is a lifestyle that is obtained through salvation and the declaration of your life being completely led by God. This goal can be easily obtained if we, as girls, walk the path of Righteousness and stand in agreement to His Word together.

G.I.R.L. : **G**ods *Intention for **R**ighteous **L**iving*

DELIVER ME FROM ME,

Sometimes I can be my worse critic, pointing out my imperfections, keeping myself bound by the lessons of my past, re-living the hurtful thoughts of my memories, being unforgiving to myself for making the wrong decisions, to others who have hurt me, or simply just not meeting the expectations I have set for myself. It can seem impossible to face the reality of my own truths, staring my situations face to face, and tackling them one by one. The only person that hurts in my world of regret is me; I've got to take hold of my current state of thinking I'm losing control. I need the strength to over-come my situations before I lose what's most valuable to me - me. I need to be delivered from the drowning thoughts of my failures, the deficiencies of my character and limitations I've placed on my future. I need to be delivered from my reminiscing day dreams that hold my freedom captive. I need to be delivered from the brutal captions my mind has placed on my memories. I need to be rescued; I need to be delivered from me!

15 Then call on me when you are in trouble, and I will rescue you, and you will give me glory. Psalms 50:15 (NLT)

Deliver Me from Me!

MY ENEMY,

Every day I barely make it. I wake up with a mind full of empty racing thoughts. I step out of bed one foot at a time, rubbing my eyes, hoping to whip away my cloudy vision. I sit still for a moment, only to try and gather my thoughts. Prioritizing my days' agenda in my head, dreading to face the chaos of this world. I count to five, 1-Lord please help me through this day, 2- I can't cry anymore tears, 3- I don't want to hurt anymore, 4- I'm so confused, 5....5 and I take a deep breath, the breath I take before I face my enemy. The breath I take before I cancel all hope I may have had for the day. The reflection of my enemy takes direction of my entire day. My enemy, let me tell you a little about my enemy. She's hurtful, she tears me down at my weakest moments, she encourages me to fail and make me feel my worse when I'm trying my very best. My enemy, she only comes around when it's time to cause pain; every day is painful. When I'm climbing to the highest mountain believing I can conquer the impossible, there she is to bring me back to reality. Reminding me of my failures, reminding me that only the beautiful can succeed. Every time I take two steps forward she knocks me back five. I just can't seem to get ahead with her around. She's been a part of my life for years, ever since I can remember. What makes things worse; I have family that encourages her and people that entice her. Let's not talk about the media; they only make her bigger, stronger and more powerful. I feel like everywhere I turn she's there, the worst thing in the world is staring into her eyes, allowing her to capture and destroy a valuable part of me. The part of me that encourages me to be the very best I can be, the part of me that compliments my originality and erases my insecurities, the part of me that takes years to build, but only seconds to destroy. Every morning I am forced to face my enemy, my choice has been taken from me, the reflection in the mirror, empty. The reflection that God created, but the enemy is holding captive, the reflection that destroys my self-esteem and has built the wall of fear around my heart, the reflection that tears my confidence apart. My enemy stares back at me through the eyes of my reflection.

My imperfections are affecting my emotional balance, causing mental anguish and self-inflicting malice. I stare deep into the color of my dark skin, hating the pigment of my layers, cutting deep in hopes to self-mend. I can't run from the truth, I can't escape my reflection, my hair isn't long enough, my waist isn't small enough according to the worlds perception. My enemy seems to be my reality, controlling my mind transforming my thoughts into a brutality, causing my actions to reflect my thoughts resulting in Christian informalities. The attacks of the enemy has my mind captured and bound, I know an idled mind is the devils playground. I've got to break free from this bondage, and escape the chase, by breaking the chains and standing up to my enemy face to face.

♥ SCRIPTURE

6 Don't worry about anything, instead pray for everything. Tell God what you need, and thank Him and for all He has done. 7 Then you will experience peace, which exceeds anything we can understand. His peace will guard your heart and minds as you live in Christ Jesus. 8...Fix your thoughts on what is true, and honorable, and right, and pure, and lovely, and admirable. Think about things that are excellent and worthy of praise.
Philippians 4:6-8(NLT)

ENCOURAGEMENT

Sometimes, we can be our worst critics, setting high expectations for ourselves, pointing out our imperfections and even comparing ourselves to those around us. We never realize that the negative things we see within us are rarely recognized by others or not as major as it seems to be. The enemy uses strategies against us to defeat us. If he can manipulate your thinking and turn you against yourself then he can use your manipulated vision to only see or even create a negative perception of yourself. God has given you power in your confession, so it is up to you to think and speak confidence into your life. By doing this, you don't give the enemy room to manipulate your thoughts of yourself. If you struggle with aligning your thinking with positive thoughts pray about it and ask God to transform your mind. Ask God to change your way of thinking, and assist you with thinking positive thoughts about yourself. After you have prayed and ask God to change the way you think about yourself, you then have to thank God for changing your thought process, even if you still have moments of discouragement, thank Him as if you're completely confident in yourself. The more you thank Him for changing your way of thinking the better your thinking will become.

Be patient this is not a 24 hour process, it will take time, patience, prayer and faith (the belief it's going to happen) to obtain the habit of positive thinking.

2 And be not conformed to this world: but be ye transformed by the renewing of your mind that ye may prove what is good, and acceptable, and perfect will of God.
Romans 12:2 (KJV)

♥ PRAYER

Dear Heavenly Father in the name of Jesus, I come to you thanking you for blessing me with another day, Lord I ask that you forgive me for any sins I have committed whether I've thought them or done them. Lord, I thank you for forgiving me for my sins. Father God, I come to you asking that you give me the ability to think positive and have good thoughts. Lord according to your Word if I transform my mind, then I may prove what is good unto you. So Lord, I ask that you transform my mind in the name of Jesus, so that I may think good thoughts about myself and my situation. Lord I thank you for changing my thoughts and I claim confidence in the name of Jesus, amen.

THE STRUGGLE,

How can I move on, you hurt me! You watched the only thing that I could call mines be taken away from me. You're supposed to protect me, love me, but all you've seem to do is destroy me. I'll never forget the day, what God created for my husband was taken from me; he laid me down as if I was his prize possession. He caressed my soul leaving the filth of his fingertips across my hopeless body. I tried to cry out, but no one heard me, no one cared, no one even noticed I had left the room. How could this be happening to me, thoughts of dismay ran through my mind? Only if I had went to school today, only if I had worn larger pajamas, only if I had cooked breakfast like he had asked, only if. My heart raced rapidly while my mind stood idol, I couldn't believe what was happening to me, I couldn't believe the man my mom called "boyfriend" was using me at his advantage. I envisioned what life would be like if I gave up mines, I can't do this, I can't take this. Please stop! My mind screamed, but my voice never made a sound. Mommy please help me, save me, rescue me from this monster, take me away and cradle me in your arms, protect me from the actions of his imagination. No one heard me, no one cared, she didn't even notice I had left the room.

I dread going back to that place, the thought of his touch makes my skin crawl. He says we're just playing a game, but this game isn't fun, it isn't fun at all. It's a daily routine, right before I go to bed each night. His footsteps are like roaring drums pouncing on the inner layers of my ears, sounding as if he were racing against the throbbing beat of my fears. I try to lie still, hoping he'll just pass bye, but my efforts to play sleep fails me each and every time. This nightmare he calls a game, feels like it lasts for hours, he touches me all over while he clinches my body closer. His grip is indescribable, there is no escape. I just lay there as he touch, feel, and fondle me, disarrayed, I patiently wait. He keeps in silence; I believe he's too ashamed to speak, while he thrusts his pelvis until he reaches his peak. He leaves my room and reminds me, it's all just a fun game, but this game isn't fun, when I'm playing against my grandfather's son.

I fight this struggle daily, I regret the day my daddy laid her down and made me! I cry out oh Lord, set free is what I declare and decree. I battle with emotional warfare a bullet thru my flesh couldn't compare the pain and anguish I struggle against, falling to me knees drowning in my tears this hate I can't resist, I'm attacked in my mind and my heart, it's hard to break these two apart. I carry unforgiveness in my soul and hate on my mind when my innocence was taken and I was forced into womanhood the only thing that stood still was time. All I could hear was the ticking of the tock but the hand never moved on my stop watch. I need an outlet, a way to escape this mess, but before I'm set free there are some things I must confess. There are many people I must forgive although it's not my heart's desire it was prepared for me in His will. His Word was created to inspire, and one day God will speak and my name is who he will admire. Proud that I meditated on His Word and overcame the obstacles the enemy set forth, casting down the walls of hatred without a doubt or remorse. I can make a list and call them name by name, but vengeance is not mines but the Lords, He will put them to shame. He said forgive them for they know not what they do, it took a spiritual break through to see this from God's point of view, but I made it, in my heart is where I saved it, the debt of those that sinned against me on the cross is where He paid it. My wrong doings and the part I played was what first I had to admit, a puddle of humiliation is where I no longer sit, walking upright in God's Word was my best fit. I had to forgive me before I forgave another; the process of spiritual growth included the forgiveness of my mother. Now she's not the only one I had to fall to my knees and pray for but she's the one who hurt me to the core. A mother's love is needed by a young girl; her love gives you the strength to conquer such an indefensible world.

I didn't call her by her name, but her title tells it all, unfortunately she is only the beginning of my spiritual pit fall. I know it wasn't my fault, but the enemies control had a tight grip. It was time to call on my prayer warriors to let it rip. I cast down the attacks of the enemy no weapon formed against me shall prosper, when God anointed me with delivering hands he created a spiritual monster. I bind up that unforgiving spirit, I will not shy down for the power of the enemy I do not fear it. The enemy can only do what it is I allowed, the fight is not conquered until God takes the bow. What I bind on earth He will bind in heaven and whatever I loose on earth He will lose in heaven, so Lord I loose the almighty spiritual seven. The confirmation of completion, finished, concluded and done this is no longer considered a struggle cause the battle is already won. Thank you, thank you, your far too kind, but you're giving the wrong person the praise and shine. I couldn't move this mountain without His mercy and grace miracles can happen but only at God's pace.

SCRIPTURE

14 If you forgive those who sin against you, your heavenly Father will forgive you. 15 But if you refuse to forgive others, your Father will not forgive your sins.
Matthew 6:14, 15(NLT)

16 Now the Lord of peace himself gives you peace always by all means. The Lord [be] with you all.
2 Thessalonians 3:16 (KJV)

6 Don't worry about anything; instead, pray about everything. Tell God what you need, and thank him for all he has done. 7 Then you will experience God's peace, which exceeds anything we can

understand. His peace will guard your hearts and minds as you live in Christ Jesus.
Philippians 4:7 (NLT)

19*Dearly beloved, avenge not yourselves, but rather give place unto wrath; for it is written, Vengeance is not mine; I will repay, saith the Lord.*
Romans 12:19 (KJV)

ENCOURAGEMENT

Many women across the world struggle with childhood molestation or rape, some even as adults are still being abused. Your situation was not experienced to tear you apart or keep you from the destiny God has planned for you. Your situation should be used to empower you and strengthen you to be a better you, to exemplify your reason of why you should succeed and be great. Being abused can inadvertently cause you to ignore or not recognize the greatness within you, but God said, that we were "fearfully and wonderfully made", therefore you were created by God on purpose and He has great plans for you. Many women who have experienced abuse tend to blame themselves in some sort of way; there is nothing you've done wrong to provoke someone to mistreat or abuse you. Use your life lesson as a strength builder and be the best you can be. I pray that you forgive your abuser and God releases peace in your heart.

139 I will praise thee; for I am fearfully and wonderfully made; marvelous are thy works; and that my soul knoweth right well.

Psalms 139:14 (KJV)

 **PRAYER**

Dear Heavenly Father in the name of Jesus, I come to you thanking you for blessing me with another day, Lord I ask that you forgive me for any sins I have committed whether thought or done. Lord, I thank you for forgiving me for my sins. Father God, I come to you asking that you release peace in my heart, Lord I have experienced hurtful things, but I know that with peace I will have the ability to endure my experience(s). Lord, according to your Word if I don't worry about the things of my past, continue to pray about my experiences and thank you for all you have done, then will you grant me peace and protect my mind as I live in you. Lord, I thank you for giving me peace; I thank you for giving me the power to forgive my abuser. I pray that you continue to harbor forgiveness in my heart so that you will continue to forgive me when I am wrong. Lord I thank you for peace and the forgiveness of my abuser and I claim victory in Jesus name, amen.

THE BULLY,

I was made a mockery. I tried buying friends, but I basically paid them to hurt me. It was tough finding friends. I didn't understand why I was chosen to live such experiences, especially at such a young age. Through all the mean people that came my way, I believe God sent me an angel. I wish I could meet him again, just to say thank you. 5th grade was hard for me, so many emotions and changes going on and no one there to help guide me through them. I tried to escape my pain by cutting myself. After my feelings became numb, the act of cutting allowed me to temporarily escape the rejections of the world. I thought I was helping myself by relieving my pain through self-mutilation. I still have the scars on my legs today. No one knew what was going on, and honestly at that moment it felt like no one even cared. They use to call me a boy, because I didn't look like them. I had to wake up every morning and face the hurtful jokes, the points, the stares and the laughter from my peers. I suffered from a disease called Polycystic Ovarian Syndrome it caused visible hair bumps on my neck and extreme pain in my abdomen. I was teased, for four consecutive years; I was emotionally abused and left with a scar. The story of my life, I wish I could hate them....but I can't!

My hurt hit like a ton of bricks, breaking me down limb by limb. Exposing my hurt to hate and blocking my heart to love. Secluding myself from the world, keeping my feelings bottled up inside, I thought all my hopes; dreams and ambitions had escaped me and died. No one was there to cheer me on or help me see through, I was left alone to battle the world and my strongest moments were only limited to a short few. I didn't quite understand why I had to experience such confronting events of life, but shortly after I was introduced to prayer I learned that every situation held a price. My story was not to break me, but to prepare me for what was near, to build me into a stronger woman and cast down every sense of fear. To hold the hand of the next girl in her time of need, guiding her through her pain and fears, because of my story, God has placed me to lead. The responsibility sounds challenging and maybe a little far fetch, who would take advice from me I haven't even overcome my own obstacles yet. It's a struggle trying to get over these hurdles, the trials and challenges of life, but how can I be an example of Christ without first living through the fight.

💜 SCRIPTURE

43You have heard the law that says, 'Love your neighbor' and hate your enemy. 44 But I say, love your enemies! Pray for those who persecute you!
Matthew 5: 43-44 (NLT)

11 "God blesses you when people mock you and persecute you and lie about you and say all sorts of evil things against you because you are my followers. 12 Be happy about it! Be very glad! For a great reward await you in heaven. And remember, the ancient prophets were persecuted in the same way.
Matthew 5:11-12 (NLT)

10 Don't be afraid, for I am with you. Don't be discouraged, for I am your God. I will strengthen you and help you. I will hold you up with victorious right hand.
Isaiah 41:10 (NLT)

"My life is an example to many, because you have been my strength and protection."
Psalms 71:7 (NLT)

ENCOURAGEMENT

Sometimes people will react to self-hurt by hurting others. Don't allow the opinions of others affect the way you view yourself. When God made you, He made no mistakes. Be confident in yourself, speak positive into your life and think wonderful thoughts of who you are and who God has called you to be. People who talk about you are searching for validation from others. They are searching for others approval to reassure them that their presence is valued, that they are important, liked or accepted. People's opinions can hurt, the phrase "sticks and stones can break my bones, but words will never hurt me" is a fabrication. Words hurt deeper than sticks and stones, a person's opinion, especially those you value, can cause you to think negatively about yourself or your situation. When you look into the mirror you have to encourage yourself, you have to keep yourself up-lifted and motivated to be the very best you can be. Your mind, appearance, color, body shape, hair length, smile, eyes, or character cannot be compared to anyone, there is no right or wrong in being who you are, the only way you're wrong is if you're being someone or something you are not!

♥ PRAYER

Dear Heavenly Father in the name of Jesus, I come to you thanking you for blessing me with another day, Lord I ask that you forgive me for any sins I have committed whether thought or done. Lord, I thank you for forgiving me for my sins. Father God, I come to you asking that you uplift my confidence according to your Word it is not meant for me to be discouraged because you are my God and you will strengthen me and help me. So Lord, I ask that you strengthen my confidence, I ask that you strengthen my self-esteem, I ask that you help me change my thinking so I can look at myself with love. Lord I thank you for strengthening my confidence and my self-esteem. I thank you for making me a better me. These things I pray in Jesus name, amen.

DELIVERANCE

Let's take a moment to learn a few ways we can help change our perception about us.

Deliverance is the act of;

- ♥ admitting you are currently in a struggle,
- ♥ understanding your current form of resolutions are not preventing you from revisiting the act
- ♥ researching scripture that identifies that it's wrong according to God (this will help you understand why it is wrong)
- ♥ praying that God delivers you from your situation according to His Word
- ♥ having the strength to fight the attacks of temptation.

 **EXAMPLE:**

Admitting the struggle:
I like having sex and I just can't seem to stop and I'm not married.

My Solutions:
- ♥ I've tried to stop, if it gets too close.
- ♥ I've tried to date guys I'm not sexually attracted too.

♥ I've tried to not be around guys at all. I masturbate so I don't want to have sex.

💜 SCRIPTURE

3For this is the will of God, even your sanctification that ye should abstain from fornication:
1Thessalonians 4:3(KJV)

19When you follow the desires of your sinful nature, the results are very clear; sexual immorality (fornication, adultery, and perversion), impurity, lustful pleasures....envy, drunkenness, wild parties, and other sin like these. Let me tell you again, as I have before, that anyone living this sort of life will not inherit the Kingdom of God.
Galatians 5:19-21 (NLT)

💜 PRAYER OF DELIVERANCE

God, I ask you to forgive me for my sins whether they were thought or done. Lord I want you to be the God of my life. I know in order for you to be the God of my life I must be delivered from the desires that will tempt me to sin. Lord I ask that you give me discipline so when I have the desire to fornicate I will have the strength to not give in. Lord, according to your Word if I cry out during my troubles you will deliver me from my distress. Lord I thank you for delivering me from my troubles of fornication, in Jesus name I pray, amen.

♥ FIGHTING THE TEMPTATION

Continue to recite the scripture above, (or whatever scripture you find pertaining to your deliverance) **Psalms 107:6**, whenever you begin to face the temptations of fornication repeat this scripture and continue to remind yourself that God will deliver you when you cry out during troubled times. Remove yourself from whatever situation that is causing you to be tempted, don't try and test yourself or God by pushing yourself to the limit, if you fail, you've made the choice to fail.

♥ STRENGTH

There is a strength that is obtained from within; it is a mental challenge that your physical body reacts to. This strength is not obtained through genetics or heredity, but through repetitious actions that build into a powerful thought

process that isn't easily distracted or destroyed;
Confidence

Strength is not just defined by physical capabilities, but also by mental and emotional challenges that requires patience, discipline and motivation to over-come life's obstacles. Situations of life can cause our strength to be amplified or diminished by the result of our decisions. You can empower your strength by enduring life's challenging situations and not allow them to defeat you. Attempting to fight the battle alone causes your struggle to be greater. Unless you make a conscious decision to seek first the Kingdom God your strength will continue to diminish the value of life one lesson at a time.

The bible says *"Seek the Kingdom of God above all else, and live righteously, and He will give you everything you need."* **Matthew 6:33 (NLT)**

Your obstacles in life are lessons to prepare you for the blessings God has planned for you, but you have to use your lessons as a process to get to Gods promises oppose to a hindrance that will keep you stagnate. God allows us to experience certain situations to strengthen us in the areas we may later need to help someone out of/or to ensure we recognize that only through Him are we able to endure. We build our endurance through life lessons. Our lessons are designed to build us into strong women of God. God only wants the best for us, He does not allow us to experience life situations without providing us instructions on how to over-come or avoid them.

8 Study this Book of Instruction continually. Meditate on it day and night so you will be sure to obey everything written in it. Only then will you prosper and succeed in all you do.
Joshua 1:8 (NLT)

Be strong in your walk, stand tall in your stride, and gracefully embrace the person God has created within you. Your strength is only as strong as you build it. The greatness of your strength is determined by your ability to allow life's obstacles be used as a building block and not as an obstruction from the vision God has designed for you. Everyday your strength grows greater according to your efforts and involvement in making you a better person. Your efforts will be pleasing unto God and He will make your efforts successful. A person is only as powerful as you allow them to be, no influence should be greater than your own. Never allow the thoughts, ideas and behaviors of those around you subject you to living an unfulfilling lifestyle.

33God is my strength and power: and he maketh my way perfect.
2 Samuel 22: 33(KJV)

29 He (God) gives power to the weak and strength to the powerless. 31 But those who trust in the Lord will find new strength...
Isaiah 40:29 (NLT)

♥ How do I build my strength?

- ♥ **Morning Prayer:** Start your day off by thanking God for the things He has done for you, then ask God to make the vision He has for you clear and obtainable.
- ♥ **Encourage yourself**: In every task you begin believe that you will produce your best, find a scripture that confirms your desire
- ♥ **Be Encouraging:** Encourage someone around you, call a friend an associate or a family member and encourage them in their day. Your encouragement could ultimately push them to be great
- ♥ **Give yourself short-term goals:** Goals that you can accomplish within 90days.

Setting these types of goals and accomplishing them will help encourage you to complete your long-term goals. It will give you a feeling of accomplishment

♥ **Identify your circle:** Surround yourself around people who can add to your strength. If the people you are associated with aren't increasing your greatness then their presence maybe hindering you from getting to where God wants you to be

My strength reflects my past, a past that carries me into tomorrow and sets the path to my future. I must not allow the things of my past cause a shift in my future. The bible says, "to worry not of the things of tomorrow for they will bring their own worries". I must build my strength daily and invest in the time it takes to have a positive perspective on WHO I am. Regardless of my surrounding influences, I will only apply the wisdom of the Holy Spirit to direct my day. My strength will come from the amount of faith I apply to my daily walk. I will trust in the Lord and make His way my objective. I will continue to strengthen my righteous living through faith, prayer, reading His Word, and obedience.

34 *"So don't worry about tomorrow, for tomorrow will bring its own worries. Today's trouble is enough for today.*
Matthew 6:34 (NLT)

Having the strength to FIGHT!

Most times in life we become defeated by our situations because we aren't equipped with the proper tools to get through them. The bible provides us with instructions on how to avoid or get through challenging situation. **Ephesians 6:10-19** teaches us how to be prepared and protect ourselves by wearing the full armor of God to fight against the attacks of the enemy.

One of our (girls) most fabulous traits is fashion; we can definitely dress up any outfit using our own form of style and taste. We dress in material clothing to be impressionable to the world but what about our spiritual fashion? The strongest woman can make rags look like riches, and the unbelievers believe.

A Righteous G.I.R.L.'s Wardrobe:

1. **High Waste Belt:** This is the Belt of truth, in all things be honest
2. **Corset:** This is your Body Armor, in all things resemble integrity and moral

3. **High Heeled Pump:** These are the Shoes of preparation, stay grounded in the Word of God, stand stern and be prepared to stand up against the enemy at any time of attack

4. **Hand Bag:** This is the your Shield of faith; we carry our handbags everywhere we go, never be without your handbag, faith holds all of your most valuable possessions, without it you are lost

5. **Cloche' Hat:** This is your hat of salvation; wear this hat earnest and proud, displaying your love of the Lord in all you do

6. **Lipstick(this is what brings your outfit together): Your Bible,** This is your Sword; read it daily, meditate on it day and night, use it to defend yourself against temptation and as instructions to live "A Righteous Lifestyle"

This wardrobe is provided to give you a better idea as to what God expects from us. These are not actual garments that are needed to be purchased, but a metaphor to help you understand the importance of wearing the full armor of God.

10A final word: Be strong in the Lord and in hid mighty power. 11 Put on all of God's armor so that you will be able to stand firm against all strategies of the devil.... 13 Therefore, put on every piece of God's armor so you will be able to resist the enemy in the time of evil. Then after the battle you will still be standing firm. 14 Stand your ground putting on the BELT of truth and the BODY ARMOR of God's righteousness. 15 For SHOES, put on the peace that comes from the Good News so that you will be fully prepared. 16 In addition to all these, hold up the SHIELD of faith to stop fiery arrows of the devil. 17 Put on salvation as your HELMET, and take the SWORD of the spirit, which is the Word of God.
Ephesians 6:10-19 (NLT)

We worry too much on our outer appearances and the fashion trends of this world. If our daily objective is to be pleasing to God, He will provide our needs and extra efforts won't be necessary. Now yes, every girl should dress as a respectful young lady, however spending too much time worrying about your appearance can cause you to idolize material things. Our main goal as Righteous G.I.R.L.'s is to be pleasing unto God not unto this world and trying to keep up with fashion trends and material collections will shift your focus. When you dress for the day, dress for the satisfaction of you not for the satisfaction of those who will see you. Being pleasing unto God will bring pleasure and others opinion will not matter.

10 *Then the way you live will always honor and please the Lord, and your lives will produce every kind of good fruit. All while, you will grow as you learn to know God better and better.*
Colossians 1:10 (NLT)

YOU ARE BEAUTIFUL!

**BEAUTY**

- ♥ **B**eing an inspiration to others
- ♥ **E**xhibiting confidence in every circumstance
- ♥ **A**iming to live a fulfilled life led by God
- ♥ **U**tilizing spiritual strength to conquer all obstacles
- ♥ **T**ransforming every negative into a positive, the power of life is in your speech
- ♥ **Y**ielding to the temptations of this world

1Peter 3:3-4 (NLT) reads: Don't be concerned about the outward beauty of fancy hairstyles, expensive jewelry, or beautiful clothes.**4**You should cloth yourselves instead with the beauty that comes from within, the unfading beauty of gentle and quiet spirit, which is so precious to God.

Now you're ready, you're equipped with helpful resources of strength building techniques. It won't be easy, but the best part of building your strength is the comfort of knowing that your strength will increase one day at a time as long as you work at it. Be patient, work diligently, study your word, be prayerful, walk by faith, and continue to confess positivity in your life and you will be as strong as the Word of God that lives within you.

DELIVER ME FROM ME,

Deliverance is not a natural motion or physical change that is immediately seen by the naked eye, but a natural decision that communicates with your spiritual being to recognize your efforts to change, then over time is seen through actions and behaviors that are contrary to your previous behaviors.

Deliverance is a decision made within your heart, it's a decision made to actively apply God's principle and wisdom to your lifestyle and change from your former way of thinking. No one can make you change; you have to feel the desire to change within your heart.

Be delivered from your past....

Be delivered from your mistakes....

Be delivered from your desires to meet the world's expectations....

FAILURE,

Why does it seem like I can never get ahead. I try so hard to be the best that I can be, but it just seems like my "good" is never good enough. It's like the world has it out for me, everyone around me seems to have it all together. I want to be somebody, I want to be successful, but I just can't seem to get over this hump. What else can I do? This thing called life is hard, I want to do better. I sit and day dream about the person I wish to become all the time, then I'm snapped back to reality by another failure, another let down. I try to get it right, but I'm always left with an empty reward that was never achieved because of my incapability to succeed. I've failed!

We're taught life isn't made up of shooting stars and fairy tales at least once, every successful person fails. But failure is nothing but an opportunity of correction, striving daily to reach the point of perfection. With his arms stretched wide, with a nail in each hand even our God was only preparing for his resurrection. When a situation seems defeated, bare through the trials and learn from the result so the misdirected idea won't be repeated. See you gotta mess up, so God can show up, to clean up, to prepare you for your move up. Success is not obtained unless faith is sustained, believing in the impossible and working towards the incredible, reaching for your highest goal making your failures inaccessible. Believing God will come without delay you must first do your part; live righteously by faith. Things don't always end the way they start, but only you can tear your dreams apart. Dream Big, conquer all, and don't be afraid, if at times you stumble and fall get back up and brush yourself off keep your focus forward only the unbelievers stay lost. Success can be a challenge, but easy don't last long so stand firm, be bold cause failure makes us strong. Strong enough to endure and patient enough to conquer and in the mist of your journey you are who God will honor.

♥ SCRIPTURE

36 *Patient and endurance is what you need now, so that you will continue to do God's will. Then you will receive all that he has promised.*
Hebrew 10:36(NLT)

8 *Study this Book of Instruction continually. Meditate on it day and night so you will be sure to obey everything written in it. Only then will you*

prosper and succeed in all you do.
Joshua 1:8 (NLT)

13 *for you will be successful if you carefully obey the decrees and regulations that the Lord gave to Israel through Moses. Be strong and courageous; do not be afraid or lose heart.*
1Chronicles 22:13 (NLT)

13 *I can do all things through Christ which strengthens me.*
Philippians 4:3(NLT)

11*Wealth from get-rich-quick schemes quickly disappears; wealth from hard work grows over time.*
Proverbs 13:1(NLT)

ENCOURAGEMENT

Failure is identified by a negative result, restricting people from the ability or desire to succeed. Throughout life we are taught that failure is a bad thing, but let's view it through a different lens. Failure gives you the opportunity to try it again; it identifies what areas need improvement and aligns you in the direction as to how to improve in the area you've failed. The only time your failure becomes a negative result is if you allow it to prevent you from trying again. Never think your dreams are too big or your expectations are too high because if you walk in the process provided by God all things are possible. Our God can do all things, but fail. We fail because we haven't yet conquered the process God has given us to reach our goal. Don't be discouraged if you fail, it may take you a couple tries before you succeed at your desire. Use small goals to encourage you to your larger goals. If you desire to open a chain of fish markets, first learn to fish. That accomplishment will encourage you to achieve your ultimate goal. The bible teaches us we can do all things through Christ who gives us strength. Meaning, there is no limit on your success, you just have to learn how to utilize the strength God has promised you, how to obtain and follow the process provided by God to get to your success through Him.

Identify your desires; ensure they are pleasing to God

Meditate on His Word so that you qualify for your promise

Apply His process to your lifestyle

Gain a clear understanding of your direction;

Imagine yourself executing your desire

Notice your spiritual growth

Elevate beyond your expectation!

IMAGINE yourself being great!

♥ PRAYER

Dear Heavenly Father in the name of Jesus, I come to you thanking you for blessing me with another day, Lord I ask that you forgive me for any sins I have committed whether thought or done. Lord, I thank you for forgiving me for my sins. Father God, I come to you asking that you provide me with the process to success. According to your Word any man that lacks wisdom let him ask so Lord I am asking that you direct me to the path of success. You said if I study and meditate on your Word both day and night then will I succeed so Lord I claim success In your son Jesus name. Lord I thank you for my success to come because I am mediating on your Word day and night. These things I ask and thank you for in Jesus name, amen.

5If you need wisdom, ask our generous God, and he will give it to you. He will not rebuke you for asking.
James 1:5(KJV)

MY APPETITE,

One meal a day, that's all I'm allowed and that meal can't stay in my belly for too long it, must come up. I carry a travel-sized toothbrush in my bag sometimes it can get a little rough. My mom has caught me a couple times but I just blame it on cramps, it works most of the time, but she just don't understand me, I can't afford to gain any more pounds. Every time I step onto the scale it ruins me. Who wants a fat girl? I can't get a boyfriend with this stomach and thighs. Do you see her shape, man I wish I could look like her; she's so beautiful and skinny. Diets, diet pills, I've tried them all, but all it does is add more weight the moment I stop. I just want to be skinny, I'd probably get more boys to like me, if I were skinny.

Don't judge me, this is how I handle my fears by expressing my uncontrollable emotion through tears. Tears that I hide so no one can ever see, so no one can ever see the true pain that lies within me. My image is holding me captive and can't let go of my grief, one day I'll be granted my wish, the life of joy and peace. I lock myself away to purge after every meal, this thing called bulimia is a disease and the life controlling symptoms are real. People think it's easy and I can just press stop at any given time, but the moment I stuck my fingers down my throat is the day I crossed the line. The line between habitual and addiction and no, the two are not the same, I could have broken my habit, but now I'm addicted and my actions have put me to shame. No one will ever know or see, the fear that dwells within me no one will ever know how strong my hate has grown beyond what the naked eye can see. No one will ever witness the pain I put myself through no one will ever see my disease cause their foot will never fit my shoe.

SCRIPTURE

3Don't be concerned about the outward beauty of fancy hairstyles, expensive jewelry, or beautiful clothes. 4 You should clothe yourself instead with the beauty that comes from within, the unfading beauty of a gentle and quiet spirit, which is so precious to God."
1Peter 3:3-4 (NLT)

ENCOURAGEMENT

Sometimes we can get so wrapped up in our image that we don't recognize that our obsessions to be beautiful are not healthy for us.

You can focus so much on your weight and or personal image that you go to the extremes to fit the world's perception of beauty. Bulimia, anorexia, diet pills, binge eating are all unhealthy habits we develop because we are trying to maintain or gain a certain appearance. Be proud of who God made you to be, if we were all created to look the same how could we ever be set apart? We were all fearfully and wonderfully made in His image and God is perfect!

♥ PRAYER

Dear Heavenly Father in the name of Jesus, I come to you thanking you for blessing me with another day, Lord I ask that you forgive me for any sins I have committed whether thought or done. Lord, I thank you for forgiving me for my sins. Father God, I come to you asking that you heal my mind from this disease that is affecting my body. Lord according to your Word whatever I bind on earth you will bind in heaven and whatever I lose on earth you will lose in heaven so Lord I bind up the addiction of bulimia, anorexia, and all eating disorders I have accumulated to try and fit in and I lose health, healthy eating, a healthy mind in the name of Jesus. Lord I as that you strengthen my self-confidence so that I will find no reason to compare myself to the images of this world. Lord you said I was created in your image and Lord you are perfect so I ask that you give me the confidence I need to encourage myself. Lord, I thank you for my confidence, I thank you for my health and I thank you for making me in your image. These things I pray in the name of your son Jesus Christ, amen.

DADDY'S GIRL,

He wasn't there for me, I needed him. I needed him to show me the love a daughter desires from her daddy. I needed him to care because in my world he was all that mattered. I needed him, I needed him to show me how my husband would one day treat me, I needed him, but he wasn't there. How can I be a queen when I was never his princess, how can I demand respect from another man when my father never showed me what I was demanding? I needed him, I needed him, but he was never there. He never told me he loved me, but my first boyfriend did, and so did the second, third, fourth and fifth. His love was the love that no other man could give me, his love was the love that would help build me into a strong powerful woman, instead I had to build myself the best way I could, I needed him, I needed him but, emotionally he wasn't there.

Who are you? A stranger with the identity of my father, struggling to build a bond that was designed to be created at birth not years after I've given birth, don't bother. Better late than never is a phrase recited by a person who didn't want you to think they had forgotten about you, but really they were struggling with conviction that reminded them of what they put you through. Who are you? You expect me to respect you and forget about the past but my memory couldn't recall when I saw you last, you've never told me you loved me or even rocked me to sleep. I wrote all my feelings in my diary, hoping one day we'd meet. To meet the man who threw me away, not once caring about how I felt, but I guess I've gotta get through this life and just play the hand I was dealt. I've found another daddy whose there for me in my time of need, and the love He has for me is, unconditionally. I want for nothing as long as I ask, He's even working with me on forgiving the hurt of my past. Yes, that includes you and the pain you've caused, but thank God for finding me cause without Him I'd be lost. I'm not the one who missed out, cause this dad is much greater, thank God He remembered me, better now than later. You'll never understand the pain or struggle I've endured; you'll never know how a daughter's wish is for her daddy to have her heart secured. To protect her from the bad guys and love her with all he has I'm try so hard to forget the past but my memory can't recall when I saw you last. I've realized I must move on with my life and not use your absence as a crutch for God has stepped in and filled the void, now I don't think of my past as much. It'll take some time but I know God will lead me through I can't keep giving that much power to a man that never cared about my point of view. I'm stronger today than I was a while back but that's because the love of my daddy is what I no longer lack!

SCRIPTURE

33 Seek ye first the kingdom of God above all else and live righteously and He will give you everything you need,
Matthew 6:33(NLT)

9" I have loved you even as the Father has loved me. Remain in my love. 10When you obey my Fathers commandments, you remain in my love, just as I obey my Fathers commandments and remain in his love."
John 15:9

10 This is real love- not that we loved God, but that he loved us as and sent his son as a sacrifice to take away our sins.
1John 4:10(NLT)

16 For God so loved the world, that he gave his only begotten son, that whosoever believeth in him should not perish but have everlasting life.
John 3:16(KJV)

ENCOURAGEMENT

Growing up fatherless can be exceptionally hard for a young woman. We expect so much out of our parents that we never take the time to understand why they do the things they do. It can be challenging to forgive your father in his absence, but let's view this situation through a different lens. Many fathers are absent from the home or are not active in their daughters lives because of fear, repeated behavior or ignorance. I've learned that being an active, full time parent is considered a choice by some fathers instead of a responsibility and when parents have made the choice to not be responsible, these behaviors are most often the result of a traumatic childhood experience they don't want to re-live. Let's use a personal experience as an example, my parents were married during my childhood, my father was in the home daily, but was not active in my life. One thing I fought to get through was I used to tell him I loved him and his response would be "Ok". That use to tear me apart until I gained the understanding of his reasoning as to why he responded to me that way, His response was developed through childhood memories of how his parents responded to him. He didn't know how to love and be affectionate to his daughters because his parents never taught him those characteristics therefore, that was all he knew. There were countless things my father did during my childhood that I never understood until I start praying and asking God for understanding. I didn't want to be mad at my father, but I couldn't help it, I felt I could have avoided many situations in my life if my father and I had a stronger relationship. We can't hold grudges in our hearts or it will cause us to block the blessing God has for us. If I had of held on to my past then God couldn't have delivered my dad and we wouldn't have gotten to the place we are today. My dad tells me he loves me every time I speak with him over the phone or see him in person.

Sometimes fathers can make bad decisions because they are afraid of taking the responsibility of being a parent, they could be afraid of failure, their father or parent wasn't active in their life, or they may just not have the understanding of how important their role is in your life. Don't harbor on the absence of your father, it is only broadening your opportunity to have an even better relationship with God. He's the best father a girl could have. I am not at all excusing the men who are not a part of their daughter's lives; I'm just leaving a little room in your heart to forgive them and to use your experience as an opportunity to grow closer to God.

PRAYER

Dear Heavenly Father in the name of Jesus, I come to you thanking you for blessing me with another day, Lord I ask that you forgive me for any sins I have committed whether thought or done. Lord, I thank you for forgiving me for my sins. Father God, I come to you asking that you renew my heart, Lord I pray that you give me the heart to forgive my father for his absence, according to your Word if I don't forgive him you won't forgive me so Lord I ask that you remove any hurt and resentment for my father from my heart. Lord I ask that you fill the empty void that my father is not present to fill. Lord, I ask that you feel the void with your love and care. Lord, I thank you for loving me; I thank you for giving me the strength and ability to forgive my father. These things I ask in your son name Jesus Christ, amen.

BAD INVESTMENT,

I've invested so much time into what I thought was my future. We were in love for the moment and everything seemed good, but then time began to settle and things began to change. Started off making life decisions as one, but remained separate individuals playing imaginary roles. I chose him, I chose him to be the father to my children and the man of my life, but not once did he ever choose me, choose me to be his wife. The energy I've invested, the time I've wasted and the words I've stressed, it only led us to argue more and love less, his long nights out were his way to escape the mess. Where did I go wrong, why didn't I see the signs? Why didn't I see that I was wasting my irreplaceable time? I thought it would be him, me, us forever, but the results of my hopeless thoughts has ended me alone and lost. With his children, our memories, and my broken heart, I must pick up the shattered piece, but our end is my new beginning and I don't know where to start.

I can't believe he left me like this; bath time, grocery shopping, doctor appointments and that's only at the top of my to-do-list. Being a mommy can sometimes have its imbalances, but being a single mother definitely carries its challenges. It's hard to move on when you started out as a team, I thought it would be us forever, or so it seemed. I invested more in you than I did in me and more in us believing it was love, and it was nothing but lust. It couldn't have possibly been love, cause love don't leave you in hurt and pain. My invested time in your confusion has caused my whole life to change; shift, move and seem a bit disarrayed, but because I stepped out of His Will this is the life I've made. I won't use it as an excuse to keep me chained and bound I'll just be sure to invest in His Word before I attempt the next round. My children are my greatest reward out of what seemed to be a mess, but next time I'll seek God first, before my heart is what I invest. This has been nothing but a life lesson, not a mistake but a blessing the couple seconds of a sex session turned my life into a lesson. The sin was the mistake, but the outcome was a blessing. I know now I must seek ye first before I make any decisions, then I know my time will be invested in the right vision.

💜 SCRIPTURE

5 Trust in the Lord with all your heart; do not depend on your own understanding. 6 Seek His

will in all you do, and He will show you which path to take.
 Proverbs 3:5-6(NLT)

22 *Whoso findeth a wife findeth a good thing, and obtaineth favor of the Lord.*
Proverbs 18:22(KJV)

8 *I will instruct thee and teach thee in the way which thou shalt go: I will guide thee with mine eye.*
Psalms 32:8(KJV)

6 *Give not that which is holy unto the dogs, neither cast ye your pearls before swine, lest they trample them under their feet, and turn again and rend you.*
Matthew 7:6 (KJV)

9 *But if we confess our sins to Him, He is faithful and just to forgive us our sins and cleanses us from all wickedness.*
1 John 1:9(NLT)

 ## Encouragement

This passage is a very sensitive subject for many women. As women, we invest in relationships that show probable cause for dismissal in early stages; however we stay in relationships expecting change because we have a natural reaction to fix what seems to look broken. By doing this we create a world of expectations, expecting our relationships to grow as one when it was never built on the proper foundation, expecting behaviors to change and habits to be broken because in our heart we're ready for commitment and marriage. These relationships result in children outside of marriage and broken hearts. Have you ever noticed after the children are born the relationship just so happen to "Not Work"? The enemy has conquered his assignment by destroying one of the sacred qualities of marriage by creating children outside of marriage. Not only has he destroyed what is designed to be shared between husband and wife, but he also has advantage over your thinking. He tries to convince you that no other man will want you and your child(dren), that's why he encourages you to stay in a relationship that you are unhappy in, to try and fix what looks to be broken in your eyes. But he isn't broken if he doesn't recognize change is needed in his life. A woman cannot change, fix or adjust the behaviors or characteristics of a man. The only person who can change man is God, and that's even according to man's will. A woman can suggest, but the ultimate decision is in the heart of man.

I encourage you to forgive yourself, and begin to invest your time into the plans and vision of God. He will direct your path and will not lead you into a pit of hurt and pain. Do not harbor on the things of previous relationships, put your trust into God and He will fulfill your every desire. When you begin to strengthen your relationship with God, He will then put you in the path of righteousness, your surroundings will change and the one He has created for you will surface. We still qualify for His promise after sin, once we repent; our sin just causes a more difficult process to obtain the promises He has for us.

♥ PRAYER

Dear Heavenly Father in the name of Jesus, I come to you thanking you for blessing me with another day, Lord I ask that you forgive me for any sins I have committed whether I thought them or done them. Lord, I thank you for forgiving me for my sins. Father God, I come to you asking that you help me make better decisions. Lord I ask that you give me the discipline to abstain from ungodly relationships and invest my time in learning and living your word. Lord, according to your word if I seek your will in all I do you will direct my path. So Lord, I ask that you conform me to the principles of your Word, so that I may apply it to my life. Lord, I know you have created a husband specifically for me, so Lord I ask that you instruct me on what I need to do for my husband to be released to me. Lord, your word says, *"any man that lacks wisdom, let him ask"* so Lord I ask that direct my path and provide me with the instructions I need to receive your promise. These things I ask in your son Jesus name, amen.

DEPRESSION,

Depression is a state of mind that controls your mental and emotional stability. Depression can be experienced at any age of life; no experience is greater than or less than the other because of age. Life situations can cause different reasons to experience depression; it is an illness that all people can be subject too. It is very controlling and will limit your ability of greatness if accepted and confessed. It takes over your emotions and causes you to feel useless, worthless, and/or less than great. It will completely discourage you from obtaining goals if accepted and confessed. The power of your confession is in your speech, if you speak negative things about yourself, your situation about your life then your results will reflect negativity.

21Death and life are in the power of the tongue; and they that love it shall eat the fruit thereof.
Proverbs 18:21

But God.....
God has given each of us the power to over-come the struggles of depression. Yes, life's obstacles can cause us to feel defeated and unworthy, however God has given us instruction on how to over-come every obstacle in life including the

idea of depression. He has given us the encouragement and the instruction on how to defeat the obstacles of life and not allow them to defeat us. He said, " *Come to me, all you who labor and are heavy-laden and overburdened, and I will cause you to rest. [I will ease and relieve and refresh your souls.]*" **Matthew 11:28(AMP)**

Depression is not a requirement of life, but a choice; we choose how we will allow our life lessons to affect our current state of mind. Dealing with the challenges in life can be overwhelming, that is why it so important to study the Word of God so that you can receive instruction on how to endure obstacles when they arise. Sometimes it may seem as if God has left your side, but He said, *"Don't be afraid, for I am with you. Don't be discouraged, for I am your God. I will strengthen you and help you. I will hold you up with my victorious right hand."* **Isaiah 41:10 (NLT)**

When obstacles arise, you can't allow it to take control of your mental state. Search scripture that provides you the process of how to overcome your struggle. Depression is state of mind that is controlled by your response to a situation. If you respond to your negative with a positive then you will have defeated one of the many obstacles that will come against you to keep you from where God has planned for you to go.

11For I know the plans I have for you, says the Lord. "They are plans for good and not for disaster, to give you a future and a hope.
Jeremiah 29:11

How do I know I need deliverance?

Again, deliverance is a natural decision that communicates with your spiritual being to recognize your efforts to change, then over time is seen through actions and behaviors that are contrary to previous behaviors. It's a spiritual discernment identifying a struggle that is preventing you from spiritual growth. You will know you are in need of deliverance when your spirit feels bound by a particular experience. If you are having difficulties with forgiving someone, forgiving yourself, loving others, loving yourself, being happy, being healthy, or anything that is inflicting emotional suffering on yourself, then you may be experiencing signs that indicate the need to be delivered.

Being delivered is not a bad thing, it is a sign that you recognize you are in a struggle and need God's guidance to pull you through.

17 The righteous cry, and the Lord hearth, and delivereth them out of all their troubles. **Psalms 34:17 (KJV)**

DELIVERANCE,

Sometimes life can deal a bold playing hand forcing us to play our next move on demand, and see, sometimes you wish you can just fold the cards you were dealt and just stop playing altogether, but that's how the enemy attempts to attack, he's far too clever. He knows our weaknesses and how to make us stumble, but in the game of life, life lessons are like fumbles, you trip over your obstacles and maybe even stagger in step, but when you recover and keep running the games not over yet. You see, you could give the enemy all control and turn over the ball, but when you're saved you are set apart and God won't let you fall. We struggle against what the world requires, but God said if we serve and obey then wealth and prosperity will transpire. Now I believe in His Word that's why I study it daily, but have you set down and had an intimate conversation with your God lately? Don't get it twisted we all have our wrongs, but he who is without sin can cast the first stone, it's one thing to do and not know, than to know and still do, but then you expect God to work miracles for you. You've got to let go of the things that are keeping you bound, peace, joy, love and happiness makes the sweetest sound. It settles your worry and soothes your storm it builds up your strength and righteousness is formed.

Deliver Me from Me!

THE DELIVERANCE PROCESS,

Step 1- Recognize your situation
When you call out your situation you are recognizing it is not of God. By doing this, will help you understand if what you are doing does not align with Gods purpose for you.
 This step will help you identify your struggle.

Step 2: Prayer
Pray to God asking for deliverance. Ask God to remove you from your situation. Ask Him to remove the hurt from your heart and then thank Him for delivering you from your situation. Remember, deliverance starts at the point of making a natural decision to change.

Step 3: Forgiveness
You have to forgive the person or people who have caused hurt and sorrow in your life. Harboring unforgiveness will only weight on your peace and could keep you from reaching God's promises to you.
14 If you forgive those who sin against you, your heavenly Father will forgive you. 15 But if you refuse to forgive others, your Father will not forgive your sins.
Matthew 6:14, 15(NLT)

Step 4 -Research Scripture

Find scripture that is relevant to your struggle. Ask God to show you in scripture how to overcome your struggle. Once you begin to seek God for wisdom, He will then begin to reveal revelation to you.

Researching scripture will strengthen you in the Word and it will help you understand your struggle and why it's important for you to overcome it.

Step 5: Attention Replacement

Replace what you are being delivered from with something positive. Begin to replace your thoughts, actions, and attention to something that is rewarding and exciting for you. Sometimes it's hard to follow through the process of deliverance because we continue to dwell on what we are supposed to be delivered from.

17 This means that anyone who belongs to Christ has become a new person. The old life is gone; a new life has begun!
2Corinthians 5:17

Step 6: Be thankful

Constantly thank God for your deliverance, thank Him for bringing you through your situation, Acknowledge His presence in your deliverance;

without Him you would still be living in your struggle.

Step 7: Walk in your deliverance

Share your deliverance with others, don't be embarrassed or shy. Your deliverance story can influence someone else's deliverance. Be bold and proud of yourself, deliverance isn't easy so be excited about where God has delivered you from.

31Get rid of all bitterness, rage, anger, harsh words, and slander, as well as all types of evil behavior. 32Instead, be kind to each other, tenderhearted, forgiving one another, just as God through Christ has forgiven you.
Ephesians 4:31-32 (NLT)

Step 8: Accountability

Hold yourself accountable, continue to be prayerful, continue to study and meditate on the Word of God so you can continue to defeat temptation and help others who are fighting their struggle.

16Confess your sins to each other and pray for each other so that you may be healed. The earnest prayer of a righteous person has great power and produces wonderful results.
James 5:16 (NLT)

UNFORGIVENESS,

Unforgiveness blocks you from your spiritual break through; it captivates the enemy's attention to repetitiously attack you. He holds your heart in bondage and form difficulties to love, he even insinuates that love doesn't exists even from our Father above. When you don't forgive another and seek revenge to harm, you open the door for the enemy to then use his strong arm, blocking you from your blessings and keeping you in captivity, never seeing the joy of life cause your mind recycles negativity. If we don't forgive those who have done wrong against us, then God will never forgive you and for eternal life that's a must. He will forgive you 7 times 70 and that's only in one day, so if you have ought against one fall to your knees, repent, and pray. Pray for your sins and those you've sinned against don't be ashamed, take your time, we all have names on our forgiveness list.

THE POWER OF A GIRL,

Today I honor all G.I.R.L.'s, girls of all shapes, sizes, and hair colors, school teachers, volunteers and especially the mothers. Girls were made strong and bold, to endure pain and hurt that no man was built to hold. A girls worth is worth far more than just a day, but today starts a national trend that recognizes that girls really do lead the way. Girls were designed to fulfill where there is lack, for the enemy knows our strength that's why we're the first he attacks, not knowing we were designed with many powers and immeasurable strengths, that's why God created WOMEN with legs of all lengths, to walk stern through the storms and stand tall in the rain only a girl can endure our history of pain. See we were designed strategically with the powers to defeat to keep the enemy up under our feet. Girls are measured by strength and we grow in numbers, faces don't need names cause once a girl has gone Righteous she is never the same.

Gods

Intentions

for

Righteous

Living!

21Whoever pursues righteousness and unfailing love will find life, righteousness, and honor.
Proverbs 21:2(NLT)

What is A Righteous G.I.R.L?

A Righteous G.I.R.L. is a person of female gender that is not recognized by age, nationality or economic status, but by the lifestyle she strives to live. The word GIRL is not used to describe an age, but a gender. I use the word "G.I.R.L." to recognize Gods Intention for Righteous Living.

A Righteous G.I.R.L. is a person of female gender who desires discipline, love, peace and joy to successfully live a Righteous lifestyle. Being "A Righteous G.I.R.L." can be declared at any age or stage of life. It is not identified by a symbol or an image, but by the example of your lifestyle.

Righteous, the act of being morally right or justifiable; virtuous showing high moral standards.

10 A Capable, intelligent, and virtuous woman-who is he who can find her? She is far more precious than jewels and her value is far above rubies or pearls.
Proverbs 31:10(AMP)

Who are Righteous G.I.R.L.'s?
A Righteous G.I.R.L.,

- ♥ Has accepted Jesus Christ as Lord and Savior
- ♥ Objective is "To Live Righteously under any circumstance"
- ♥ Comes in all different shapes, sizes, ages, colors, nationalities, personalities, styles, fashions and images
- ♥ Possess confidence and ambition in God's purpose for herself
- ♥ Is identified by her gifts and talents not by the way she dresses
- ♥ Only allow positive speech to flow from her tongue
- ♥ Carry's herself as a lady at all times
- ♥ Is clothed in strength and dignity
- ♥ Spreads the gospel to girls of all categories
- ♥ Understands her faults and repents for her mistakes
- ♥ Is energetic, strong and hard working
- ♥ Encourages and strengthens other girls spiritually and emotionally
- ♥ Fears the Lord

I WANT TO BE "A Righteous Girl"

Pray the prayer of Salvation,

Heavenly Father in the name of your son Jesus Christ, I am ready to live my life according to your Word. I am ready to be your daughter and inherit the promises of your Word. Please forgive me for all of my sins, the ones I have thought and the ones I have done. Lord you said in your Word if I confess with my mouth that Jesus is Lord and believe in my heart that you raised him from the dead then I will be saved. So God I confess with my mouth and believe in my heart that you raised your son Jesus Christ from the dead and now I AM SAVED. Lord, I ask that you guide my heart and mind so that I may begin to live a righteous lifestyle. Lord, I accept you as my Lord and Savior Jesus Christ. These things I pray in the name of your son Jesus Christ, amen.

♥ You are now "A SAVED Righteous Girl"!

A RIGHTEOUS G.I.R.L. PRAYER,

Lord, I ask that you welcome me into your presence with a pure mind and pure heart. I ask that you forgive me for what I have said, done, or thought that was against your word.

Lord I come to you today asking that you direct my path and manifest my purpose. Lord lead me into righteousness; continue to help me make righteous a lifestyle. I pray that your anointing covers me, protects me from the attacks of this world and help me to make righteous decisions. Lord I pray for my enemies and those who have done wrong against me, I ask that you bless them and give them the desires of their hearts.

In Jesus Name I Pray, Amen

16...The earnest prayer of a righteous person has great power and produces wonderful results.
James 5:16 (NLT)

I AM, A Righteous G.I.R.L.

A Righteous Girl, striving daily to rebuke the devours of the world. Waking up with Christ on my heart, seeking God first is how a blessed day starts. Lord I ask that you forgive me for my sins, I must forgive an unforgiver, may the best girl win. I step into my shoes of confidence, to walk ambitiously on my path of my purpose, defeat or failure for me, God's child, I'm impervious. I gladly follow the footsteps of the righteous, the benefit and reward of a believer is priceless. Meditate on His word daily, have you measured the power of your faith lately? For I can do all things through Christ who gives me the strength; God's favor and my obedience is beyond measurable lengths. He said He'll pour you out blessings you won't have room to receive, don't take my word for it, watch my lifestyle, I won't have to force you to believe. I clothe myself in strength and in dignity, for my reward, God has granted me immunity, against poverty, sadness, depression and regret it's from the walk of my path that changes the effect. See, I don't want for anything cause God will supply all my wants and my needs, and I don't live in sadness cause spreading God's word is my hearts passion. I can't be depressed cause I'm not oppressed by the things of this world, Jesus Christ is my savior and He is who I call Lord. How can you live in regret if you didn't go through what you've been through, you wouldn't have a reason to push forward. You can compare the value between a ruby and a pearl but true riches rest in the heart of A Righteous Girl.

"A Righteous G.I.R.L." is a state of mind, it's a firm decision to walk righteously, it's the desire and ability to live a Righteous Lifestyle; any girl can be "A Righteous G.I.R.L."!

G*ods* **I***ntention for* **R***ighteous* **L***iving!*

♥   Toya

MY DELIVERANCE CHECKLIST:

Here's your very own deliverance check list. Let's make sure you're equipped to release those things that have happened in your past that has caused you to slow down your spiritual growth. Use the space provided to write your situation. Writing it out will encourage you during your process; it will hold you accountable to your decision to change.

☐ I have recognized my struggle and understand how it does not align with God's purpose for me.

_____ Date

_____

_____

_____

_____

_____

_____

_____

_____

☐ I have prayed and asked God to deliver me from my situation. I will no longer allow my past experiences to interfere with my spiritual growth.

_____ Date

_____

_____

_____

_____

_____

_____

_____

_____

_____

_____

_____

_____

_____

☐ I have forgiven the following people who have caused hurt in my life. I have also prayed and asked God to forgive me.

_____ Date

_____

_____

_____

_____

_____

_____

_____

_____

_____

_____

_____

_____

_____

☐ I have researched scripture that help me over-come my struggle.

_____ Date

_____

_____

_____

_____

_____

_____

_____

_____

_____

_____

_____

_____

_____

_____

☐ I have replaced hurtful thoughts and memories of my past with things that make me happy and excited.

_____ Date

_____

_____

_____

_____

_____

_____

_____

_____

_____

_____

_____

_____

_____

_____

☐ I am thankful for my deliverance. Thank you God, for my deliverance.

_____ Date

_____

_____

_____

_____

_____

_____

_____

_____

_____

_____

_____

_____

_____

☐ I walk proudly in my deliverance. I want to share my story with the world. I am bold and proud of where God has brought me from.

_____ Date

_____

_____

_____

_____

_____

_____

_____

_____

_____

_____

_____

_____

I must hold myself accountable for my deliverance. I have written it down, and will read it daily. I will encourage myself to continue to stride for greatness! I am will be great, I am great!

_____ Date

_____

_____

_____

_____

_____

_____

_____

_____

_____

_____

_____

_____

_____

YOUR DELIVERANCE,

You were wonderfully and fearfully made in His image and I pray that God gives you peace in your struggle. God has created you to be great and I pray that your confession begins to speak greatness. Life can be challenging, but God has made you strong enough to conquer your struggle. A struggle is designed to strengthen your ability to get through and be great. Don't doubt yourself, believe that God made you on purpose with a purpose, now let go of your past and fulfill your purpose.

You are amazing, and I love you!

♥   Toya, xoxo

ABOUT THE AUTHOR,

LaToya Early, wife, woman of God, mother of two, writer and business owner. LaToya is a Detroit native where she attended Detroit Public Schools and Oakland University in Rochester, Michigan. She is a faithful servant of the Kingdom of God at Fountain of Truth Church in Detroit, Michigan where she is pro-vision to the vision God has given her spiritual parents. She is a prominent servant of their youth ministry, Righteous Youth Church where she is operating under God's anointing and spiritual gifts to serve.

LaToya is founder of a girl's ministry "A Righteous G.I.R.L" that is designed to empower and encourage young women of all ages to live a Righteous lifestyle. A Righteous G.I.R.L was created under the teachings of Righteous Youth Church, where the vision is to transform the lives of youth. ARG is available to young women across the nation; it is not a place or a location, but simply a way of living.

Any girl can be "A Righteous G.I.R.L."!

A Righteous G.I.R.L.
(Gods Intention for Righteous Living)
www.Arighteousgirl.com

"I have had the desire to write since I was a young girl, thriving for the opportunity to provide words of encouragement and wisdom to young women across the world. Being an author, to me, is God's way of assigning me to minister His Word through writing. May this reading save, deliver and transform the lives of millions."

Mrs. LaToya Early,
♥ Be Blessed xoxo

Published by: MBC Publishing

Scripture quotations noted KJV are from the Holy Bible, King James Version © 2010 by online Bible at youVersion.com

Scripture quotations noted NLT are from the Holy Bible, King James Version © 2010 by online Bible at youVersion.com

Scripture quotations noted AMP are from the Holy Bible, King James Version © 2010 by online Bible at youVersion.com

Editor: Naima Gibson, Tamara Thorpe. Kaela Ritter, Paris France

Cover Design: NG Designs and Prints

Interior Design: LaToya Early, Ken Jones

Printed in: The United States of America